The Poetry
of Norman MacCaig

Roderick Watson

Association for Scottish Literary Studies 1989

Published by
Association for Scottish Literary Studies
Scottish Literature
7 University Gardens
University of Glasgow
Glasgow G12 8QH

www.asls.org.uk

ASLS is a registered charity no. SC006535

First published 1989
Reprinted 1999, 2000, 2001, 2003,
2004, 2006, 2008, 2011

© Roderick Watson

A CIP catalogue for this title is available
from the British Library

ISBN: 978 0 948877 07 0

The Association for Scottish Literary Studies
is in r~~~i~t ~f ~~h~id~ fr~m Cr~~tiv~ S~~tland

Glasgow Life Glasgow Libraries	
Schools	
005558591	
Askews & Holts	08-Jan-2014
821.914 ⟍	£5.50

Typeset by Roger Booth Associates, Hassocks, West Sussex
Printed by Bell & Bain Ltd, Glasgow

SCOTNOTES

Study guides to major Scottish writers and literary texts

Produced by the Education Committee
of the Association for Scottish Literary Studies

THE ASSOCIATION FOR SCOTTISH LITERARY STUDIES

aims to promote the study, teaching and writing of Scottish literature, and to further the study of the languages of Scotland.

To these ends, the ASLS publishes works of Scottish literature; literary criticism and in-depth reviews of Scottish books in *Scottish Literary Review*; short articles, features and news in *ScotLit*; and scholarly studies of language in *Scottish Language*. It also publishes *New Writing Scotland*, an annual anthology of new poetry, drama and short fiction, in Scots, English and Gaelic. ASLS has also prepared a range of teaching materials covering Scottish language and literature for use in schools.

All the above publications are available as a single 'package', in return for an annual subscription. Enquiries should be sent to:

ASLS
Scottish Literature
7 University Gardens
University of Glasgow
Glasgow G12 8QH

Tel/fax +44 (0)141 330 5309
e-mail **office@asls.org.uk**
or visit our website at **www.asls.org.uk**

CONTENTS

EDITORS' FOREWORD

The *Scotnotes* booklets are a series of study guides to major Scottish writers and literary texts that are likely to be elements within literature courses. They are aimed at senior pupils in secondary schools and students in further education colleges and colleges of education. Consequently it is intended that, wherever possible, each booklet in the series will be written by a person who is not only an authority on the particular writer or text but also experienced in teaching at the relevant levels in schools or colleges. Furthermore, the editorial board, composed of members of the Schools and Further Education Committee of the Association for Scottish Literary Studies, considers the suitability of each booklet for the students in question. In preparing the series, the editors are conscious of the fact that for many years there has been a shortage of readily accessible critical notes for the general student of Scottish literature; and they intend that *Scotnotes* will grow as a series at the rate of about two booklets a year to meet this need and provide students with valuable aids to the understanding and appreciation of the key writers and major texts within the Scottish literary tradition.

Lorna Borrowman Smith
Alan MacGillivray

NOTE ON REFERENCES

All page references in this study guide are to Norman MacCaig, *Collected Poems* (London, 1985).

THE POET: ' ... MAKING SOMETHING THAT WAS NEVER IN THE WORLD BEFORE'

Norman MacCaig does not like to speak about himself. As one of Scotland's best known writers, appreciated by audiences all over the country, he is still a private man with a self-confessed 'hundred horsepower revulsion from writing about myself'.[1] Nor does he care for the notion, so fashionable in the sixties, that poetry is a form of therapeutic personal 'confession', or that 'the times being what they are, the only poetry possible is a poetry of extremes, scribbled frantically on your way back from a mental hospital to commit suicide'.

Of course MacCaig recognises that there are poems to be written 'from the far edge of consciousness, of suffering, of despair', and he has sometimes been there himself. But there are many other poems written simply for the pleasure of reading them, or of making them, 'and [this] seems to me not different from a true craftsman's pleasure in making a table, or a meal to put on it, or a boat that marries the water as a boat should. The pleasure in making something that was never in the world before, with our gifts and abilities at their farthest stretch, is surely one that is common to everybody'. These words might make poetry seem to be quite a modest thing, but they also allow it to be central to ordinary human experience and hence accessible to us all.

MacCaig's personal reticence and his sense of pleasure and modest celebration in writing poetry take us to the heart of his work. The witty elusiveness with which he speaks about his craft should not blind us to the depths of insight which can lie behind even his simplest poem.

Born in Edinburgh in 1910, Norman MacCaig has spent all his working life in that city, going from the Royal High School to the University in 1928, and graduating four years later with an Honours degree in Classics. He trained as a school teacher and followed this profession for most of his life. He and his wife Isabel were married in 1940 and they have two children. A deeply held personal conviction against the act of killing led him to become a conscientious objector during the Second World War, and he passed the war years in non-military work.

Norman MacCaig's first poems were published in a number of periodicals in the 30s and 40s, and collected in two books

called *Far Cry* (1943), and *The Inward Eye* (1946). At this time
he was reckoned to be an 'Apocalyptic' writer, one of a small
group who set out to find personal inspiration and even reve-
lation in their poems, as if this were something positive to set
against what they felt to be the spiritual and material chaos of
the war years. Henry Treece (later known for his historical
novels) was one of the founders of this short-lived movement,
along with Scotsmen G.S. Fraser and J.F. Hendry. MacCaig,
then in his thirties, and the younger Tom Scott were associated
with these and other writers in 'the New Apocalypse' anthol-
ogies, with poems full of strange symbols and surrealist images
and densely packed language — not unlike the first verses of
Dylan Thomas, which had appeared in the 1930s.

MacCaig has since disowned this early work, although his
life-long interest in landscape was there from the start. He may
refer to some mysterious 'stone noose' and 'the way in crystal',
but he also enjoys 'the fabulous narration of the air / and the
hoarse lyrics of heather and bog-myrtle'.[2] Nevertheless, he
came to reject such lines as too wilfully obscure, 'rescued', he
remembers, 'by the only critical remark that was ever any use
to me, when my second book came out and a friend, having
read it, handed it back to me, saying, "When are you publishing
the answers?" This took me several steps back towards my
senses and I started on the long haul towards lucidity'.

With his first two books behind him, it is *Riding Lights*,
from 1955, which marks the beginning of MacCaig's mature
work. 'Summer Farm' (15), a much-anthologised poem from
that volume, demonstrates his new lucidity and a characteristic
way of looking at things. The poem begins with a few well-
chosen small details. It seems to be a hot day. Notice how the
writer concentrates on simple numbers, with *nine* ducks in *two*
lines.

> Straws like tame lightnings lie about the grass
> And hang zigzag on hedges. Green as glass
> The water in the horse-trough shines.
> Nine ducks go wobbling by in two straight lines.

At first he seems to be merely a passive observer, quietly amazed
at what he finds around him:

> A hen stares at nothing with one eye,
> Then picks it up. Out of an empty sky
> A swallow falls and, flickering through
> The barn, dives up again into the dizzy blue.

> I lie, not thinking, in the cool, soft grass,
> Afraid of where a thought might take me — as
> This grasshopper with plated face
> Unfolds his legs and finds himself in space.

Everything seems so obvious and simple. Like so many good poems, it makes us recognise what we have all seen — ducks waddling, a hen pecking the ground — even if we couldn't have said it quite like that. But there are odder things going on as well.

There's a suggestion of emptiness — with a swallow *falling*; with the sky being 'dizzy blue', and with that grasshopper suddenly *finding itself* in *space*. All these, when we begin to notice them, somehow make the setting seem less familiar. As a matter of fact, the image of a sparrow flying through a barn is used in Anglo-Saxon literature to symbolise how tragically fleeting human life is, but even without knowing this, there is still something disturbing about the poet being 'afraid of where a thought might take me', as if he, too, might find himself suddenly out in space or up in the 'dizzy blue'.

And then MacCaig recognises that he is not just a passive observer, but that there's always something at least half creative in the way we choose to see the world. However impartial we think we are being when we describe something, somewhere within our description, there's a little bit of ourselves as well. This always happens in art, and in fact it's an inescapable part of any form of expression. We cannot step outside our own skins. MacCaig writes as if he and the poem and his sense of himself were like a string of beads, each mirroring and leading on to the next (just as the rhyme scheme reflects itself), or like a set of concentric Chinese boxes. Thus everything is reassuringly connected or enclosed after all. This is how the poem ends:

> Self under self, a pile of selves I stand
> Threaded on time, and with metaphysic hand
> Lift the farm like a lid and see
> Farm within farm, and in the centre, me.

Justly famous, 'Summer Farm' is typical of Norman MacCaig's poetry and of what were early recognised as his special qualities of wit, clarity, restraint and lively first-hand observation. At the age of 45, the mature poet had come into his own.

Edinburgh was an exciting place to be during the 1940s and 50s, for a number of Scottish poets were living in the city at this time and there are many accounts of them holding deep

discussions in the Café Royal, or relaxing in Milne's Bar and
other establishments in Rose Street, a not-so-royal mile famous
for its old-fashioned bars and howffs. This period marks what
has been called the second wave of the 'Scottish Literary Renaissance' — that revival of confidence in writing and publishing
which began with Hugh MacDiarmid in the early twenties. It
was in Edinburgh that MacCaig also cemented a lifelong friendship with MacDiarmid, despite their many differences of opinion.
The elder poet recognised that MacCaig was very different from
himself — being 'apolitical or anti-political' — but he still held
him to be 'almost the only fellow-writer . . . with whom I can
have a really serious discussion on literary, or other intellectual
and artistic matters'.[3] Sidney Goodsir Smith, Robert Garioch,
Tom Scott, Alexander Scott and Sorley MacLean also became
friends, along with so many other writers in subsequent years,
for the MacCaigs were 'the most generous of hosts', as Mac-
Diarmid acknowledged, and their flat became a special 'rendez-
vous for congenial spirits from far and near'.

After *Riding Lights*, thirteen more collections of MacCaig's
poetry were published, until the large *Collected Poems* appeared
in 1985. His professional life progressed quietly and he con-
tinued to teach in Edinburgh during these years, spending
every summer at Inverkirkaig, near Lochinver on Scotland's
north west coast, where he loves to fish among the hill lochs.
In 1967 he was appointed for two years as Edinburgh University's first Fellow in Creative Writing, talking to student poets
and helping other budding writers with their work. He became a
headmaster in 1969, and then in 1970 he joined the Depart-
ment of English Studies at the University of Stirling, first as a
lecturer, and then as Reader in Poetry where he held tutorials
and worked as a regular member of staff until his retirement in
1978. Norman MacCaig has received many awards, including an
OBE and the Queen's Medal for Poetry. In reading his work
aloud, with his own memorably witty and dry presentation, he
has become well-known on radio and television, and much
appreciated by audiences in literary societies and schools throughout Britain.

' . . . for half my thought and half my blood is Scalpay'

Biographical details, more often than not, fail to reveal
much about a poet's inner creative life. This is certainly true of
MacCaig, not least because he has been so very reluctant to

write about himself. But he has acknowledged one key influence over the years, and this has to do with his family's roots in the Western Highlands and Islands of Scotland. His mother came from Scalpay, Harris, in the Outer Hebrides, and this Gaelic inheritance has been very important to him, even if he does not speak Gaelic, having been born in Edinburgh where his mother came to live with her Lowland Scots husband.

It is as if MacCaig has always been balanced between two worlds: he spends his summers in the Highlands, but lives and works in the city. He writes with what he takes to be a Gaelic clarity, but he does it in English. He loves pibroch, the classical music of the Highland bagpipe, but he loves the music of Mozart, too. The poet confronted this division in 'Return to Scalpay' (264):

> Scalpay revisited? — more than Scalpay. I
> Have no defence,
> For half my thought and half my blood is Scalpay,
> Against that pure, hardheaded innocence
> That shows love without shame, weeps without shame,
> Whose every thought is hospitality —
> Edinburgh, Edinburgh, you're dark years away.

MacCaig remembered his Edinburgh childhood in 'Inward Bound', but beyond those early days he is still aware of Scalpay, and even Gaelic, as an equal force — however distant — in his memories and his inheritance:

> Out of my speech
> I trespassed over the border
> into Gaelic and glimpsed
> facts and the decoration of facts
> that now only glimmer in my mind
> like a coin at the bottom of a well.   (250)

Such facts and their 'decoration' relate to the formal and restrained way that Gaelic poetry describes nature, and MacCaig associates this with the same impulse in his own work, as he once explained in a rare autobiographical essay which he called 'My Way of It':

> A man, whether he like it or not, can't climb down from his genealogical tree and scramble up another of his own choice. To go back, then, only two generations, three of my grandparents were Gaels and the fourth was a Border Scot from Dumfriesshire. She's the one who gets me to places on time.

I am, that's to say, a threequarter Gael. Now, Celtic art is not
at all the romantic, not to say sentimental thing of popular belief.
Its extreme formality is to be seen in all the forms it takes — in its
carvings and sculptures, its personal ornaments, its poetry and
its music. (Think of pibroch.) All those genes I carry about, therefore, incline me strongly towards the classical rather than the
romantic, the Apollonian rather than the Dionysian, and this
inclination was both revealed and supported by the fact that I
took a degree in Classics. By some, sloped in the other direction,
my work has at times been criticised as being, to their taste, too
cool, too restrained, too controlled. Naturally this doesn't bother
me at all. My defence, if I were to make one, would be restrained
murmurings about the distinction between passion and emotion
and a smug re-telling of Mallarmé's answer to the lady who asked
him, 'Do you not, then, ever weep in your poetry, Monsieur
Mallarmé?' 'No, madame,' he said, 'and I don't blow my nose in
it either'.

As a 'threequarter Gael' who lives in Edinburgh, MacCaig
finds himself with what he calls 'binocular vision', for even as
he walks round the Highlands in the poem 'Centre of centres',
there come to him flashes from his other life in the city:

> I see like a bird or a fish,
> a boat with one eye a bus with the other,
> a crofter left a traffic warden right:
> a supermarket ghosts up
> from the shallows of Loch Fewin
> and round the foot of Suilven
> go red deer and taxis.   (235)

This is not a schizophrenic split (although with a different writer
it could be) for MacCaig's experience as a poet has always been
to find himself in the centre of many circles as he moves through
life. They can be predictable or unpredictable, historical or
immediately present, but he always tries to balance them
against each other:

> How many geometries are there
> with how many circles
> to be a centre of?
> As though a man, alive in his imagination,
> trips on this stone and stumbles
> on the field of the Battle of the Braes or, walking

to Murrayfield, is one of a crowd
moving in silence
to the execution of Montrose.

I name myself, I name this place, I say
I am here; and the immediacies
of the flesh and of the reports
of its five senses (I welcome them)
make their customary
miraculous declarations, from which
all else falls away.   (235-6)

This takes us back again to 'Summer Farm', when we saw
the poet naming yet another circle only to find 'farm within
farm, and in the centre, me'. MacCaig has always had respect for
the 'miraculous declarations' to be found in everyday reality —
if only we can open our eyes to them, for '. . . of course one is
influenced by, simply, everything. For the senses, the "five
ports of knowledge", are hospitable to everything, and into
them sail, with luck, the most remarkable cargoes'.[4]

'Noticing' and 'Balancing'

I said that MacCaig's impulse is to 'balance' things in his
poems, and for the most part he takes a great delight in what
the world brings to him. But there are times when the contra-
dictions are too great for even the wittiest of his metaphors, and
he struggles under the burden of a world in which beauty and
horror, music and torture can exist side by side. The poem
'Equilibrist' speaks quite frankly about such moments, and
offers a rare insight into the man and his work. It is worth quoting in full.

Equilibrist

I see an adder and, a yard away,
a butterfly being gorgeous. I switch the radio
from tortures in foreign prisons
to a sonata of Schubert (that foreigner),
I crawl from the swamp of nightmare into
a glittering rainfall, a swathing of sunlight.

Noticing you can do nothing about.
It's the balancing that shakes my mind.

What my friends don't notice
is the weight of joy in my right hand
and the weight of sadness in my left.
All they see is MacCaig being upright,
easy-oasy and jocose.

I had a difficulty in being friendly
to the Lord, who gave us these burdens,
so I returned him to other people
and totter without help
among his careless inventions.   (331)

— So there is a darker side to the 'remarkable cargoes'
brought home by our senses from the world at large. And Mac-
Caig must face this darkness on his own, because he does not
believe in God, and will not use Christian faith to explain things
or to make them easier to bear. In the poet's eyes, God is like
some 'absentee landlord ... lounging by his infinite swimming
pool', planning to visit the sins of the fathers on the children
('The Kirk', 332). Even so, he still finds much to praise among
those 'careless inventions' all around us, and for the most part
they bring him a saving sense of pleasure and delight, and spiritual refreshment too. As an artist Norman MacCaig has a special
and consistent impulse towards celebration, and it is this which
brings us now to the poems themselves.

THE POEMS: 'REMARKABLE CARGOES'

There is a long tradition of 'praise poems' in Gaelic culture. From ancient bardic times until well into the 16th century, verses were composed — or commissioned — in praise of famous chiefs, warriors and battles, or of handsome men, beautiful women and skilled poets or musicians. Places of local interest or beauty were celebrated too, and by the eighteenth century a tradition of nature poetry had grown up, less formal and bardic in expression, but full of specific detail and the kind of glittering precision which MacCaig has admired so much for refusing to be the least bit romantic or sentimental. Among the most famous of these poets are Alasdair MacMhaighstir Alasdair (1695?-1770?), who wrote 'Song to Summer', 'Sugar Brook' and 'Clanranald's Galley'; and Duncan Ban Macintyre (1724-1812), who immortalised the deer, hillside grasses and pools of his favourite mountain, in poems such as 'Praise of Ben Dorain' and 'Song to Misty Corrie'. A few lines from 'Misty Corrie' (translated by Angus MacLeod) will show something of what MacCaig sees as the objective and 'classical' spirit of Gaelic poetry:

> In the rugged gulley is a white-bellied salmon
> that cometh from the ocean of stormy wave,
> catching midges with lively vigour
> unerringly, in his arched, bent beak,
> as he leapeth grandly on raging torrent,
> in his martial garb of the blue-grey back,
> with his silvery flashes, with fins and speckles,
> scaly, red-spotted, white-tailed and sleek.[5]

Norman MacCaig doesn't use Gaelic, and his voice is more informal than Duncan Ban's, nevertheless many of his poems are 'praise poems' in this tradition. Over and over again they celebrate landscape and the ordinary people to be found in it, and above all, the other living creatures — animals, fishes and birds — whose space we share.

' . . . pure celebration'

Writing in 'My Way of It', the poet regrets that 'a great part' of modern poetry has been written to express personal despair and 'inner psychological tensions'. In place of this he makes a plea for the other 'great part' of art:

> ... whose cause, purpose and effect is pure celebration of a
> woman or a chair or a landscape? Are we to dismiss these as
> trivial? If so, I have written a good many trivial poems, and
> here's one.

> *Ringed plover by a water's edge*
>
> They spring eight feet and —
> stop. Like that. They
> sprintayard (like that) and
> stop.
> They have no acceleration
> and no brakes.
> Top speed's their only one.
>
> They're alive — put life
> through a burning-glass, they're
> its focus — but they share
> the world of delicate clockwork.
>
> In spasmodic
> Indian file
> they parallel the parallel ripples.
>
> When they stop
> they, suddenly, are
> gravel.   (267)

The poet concludes: 'In my self-belittling way I call poems of
this kind (they're really celebratory) "snapshot poems", a bad
habit I keep meaning to break'.

'Snapshot' or not, these lines make a fine poem in praise of
everything that is special about how a plover moves and looks.
They may seem simple and straightforward — this is a free verse
poem, after all, with no rhyme scheme and no regular rhythmical
structure — but a lot of subtle effects and connections are being
made beneath the surface. With the lines re-set as prose the
'sense' of the piece is perfectly straightforward:

> They spring eight feet and stop like that. They sprint a yard like
> that and stop. They have no acceleration and no brakes. Top
> speed's their only one. . . . etc.

(Try setting down any free verse poem as prose, and then re-organise the lines in your own style. It's an exercise which shows how much more can be expressed by laying out the words on the page in a particular way. MacCaig himself changed over to free verse with *Surroundings* in 1966. Actually, he believes that it is *more* difficult 'to write a formally good poem in free verse . . . than to mosaic away with iambs and feminine rhymes'.)

What the layout of 'Ringed plover . . . ' offers us is 'sprintayard' run together; and a whole line given over to a single word, 'stop'; while the second line, too, is broken up into short, sudden, isolated words:

> stop. Like that. They

— All this does much to make us feel the sudden rush and halt of how the bird habitually moves. Are there other effects like this?

Well, 'In spasmodic / Indian file' is broken up in the same way, only to be followed by a line which is twice as long, with its own peculiar, liquid, tongue-twisting sound. And what about the very *shape* of those words: 'parallel' and 'ripples'? And why repeat 'parallel'?

The last section uses abrupt punctuation again with its line 'they, suddenly, are'; but what does this last section mean? How can the birds *be* gravel? Is it their colour? Or their stillness? Are they now dead or unfeeling, *like* gravel? — And why ask all these questions? This may be a useful point to talk about in deciding how to read MacCaig's poems.

A word about method

In responding to poetry, we have to notice things on the printed page just as sharply as the poet notices things in the real world. Asking questions as I have been doing is just a way of directing attention to what is there before us all the time. The trick, of course, is to ask the right questions. Once asked, however, the answers start to come thick and fast, and they should be drawn out of your own experience and thoughts. (That's why I won't always answer my own questions in this guide.)

In this particular case, it seems to me that when the birds stop *moving* they merge into the gravel of the shore; but also when they stop *living* they will become part of the landscape, cold and dead like stone. Some readers will prefer one explanation, others another, and some will accept two or more different readings at the same time. So it is that, in a sense, each of us assembles the poem for ourselves out of our own reading and experience and according to what we notice on the page. This is how poetry (and all art, in fact) comes alive in a unique way, special to each of us. It's an inter-active process, to which we too, and not just the artist, must have something to contribute. In this special sense a poem in a closed book doesn't really exist. Like a painting in a dark room, it may be *there* alright, but as a work of art — that is, as a work of *communication* — it is not yet alive.

This isn't an invitation to seek far-fetched things in a simple poem, nor is it a licence to say that a poem can mean anything we want it to mean, because in the end we must stay true to common sense and what is actually printed on the page, so that whatever is found there, it should fit in with everything else in the poem, taken as a whole. We discover what's convincing and what's not by talking to each other (or even to ourselves) and by coming back to the same lines at a later date to think again. (In fact, poems are a concentrated form of literary expression, specially designed for reading more than once in just this way.) Now to return to that plover at the water's edge and a final — slightly more difficult — question.

What about the middle four lines, and, in particular, what does MacCaig mean when he says that the birds 'share the world of delicate clockwork'?

I think the key here is to notice that the poet is saying in effect that the plovers are alive, but move like clockwork — i.e., something not alive. The images used here are quite striking because he calls up the mechanical movements of inanimate machinery — 'delicate clockwork' — only to set them against life itself which is visualised as if it were a spot of sunshine through a magnifying glass. So life is something intangible *made* tangible, just as sunlight (seen but not 'seen' everywhere) can be focused down to an intense spot of light and heat. Yet these birds are also jerky and frail, like little machines. This is why, for myself, I get just the slightest hint of death at the very end of the poem, because using the word 'stop', so soon after talking about a piece of clockwork suggests something halted or perhaps with its time run-down in a more final sense.

One of the freedoms that free verse allows a poet to take is to model his lines so that they imitate or enact what's being described, and in this poem, as in so many others, MacCaig takes pleasure in the craft. But the *point* of the poem is to make vivid what's special about plovers, as if we had never seen one before (and maybe we haven't). Even if we do know all about plovers, the poem makes us see them again, freshly and surprisingly, as if for the first time. Whether in prose, poetry or painting, one of the things that art does is to 'celebrate' the ordinary in just this way, by revealing it as something not so ordinary, after all.

Animals and metaphors

For MacCaig, the natural world has always been special, and in particular the world of animals. Their unique movements, their oddity, their charm and (often) their small scale, all seem to stimulate the best qualities of the poet's observation, his dry wit and an unsentimental compassion. Here he can celebrate the variety and the modest sturdiness of life, without the problems which self-awareness and the promptings of the ego so often bring to human affairs. MacCaig has written about collie dogs, cows, bulls, horses, goats, deer and, most especially, birds of every description. Hens, ducks, pigeons, crows, blackbirds, starlings, sparrows, wrens, blue tits, bullfinches, stonechats, greenshanks, waxwings, grey wagtails, plovers, gulls, cormorants, puffins, kingfishers and swans all feature in what are often his best-known and best-loved poems, not to mention porpoises, sharks, whales, caterpillars, earwigs, lizards, toads and, on several guest appearances, frogs.[6]

MacCaig's art is to make us re-experience his own reactions of surprise and delight when confronted with yet another of creation's 'marvellous inventions', and the opening line of 'Toad' (336), is a good example. 'Stop looking like a purse' throws us into the middle of things, as if the toad were in front of us and the poet already talking to it. The metaphor is more startling still, for the sudden connection between a toad's slack and paunchy body and one of those old-fashioned snap top purses goes off like a flash bulb in the reader's brain. The link is at the same time far-fetched and absolutely convincing.

Metaphor in poetry always works like this — by describing one thing in terms of another thing. But the distance between these two things ('toad' and 'purse') must be just right for the poem to work well. If they are too far apart ('toad stop looking like an orange'), we're simply puzzled; and if they're too close, ('toad stop looking like a frog'), then there's no magic to the line at all.

Once again we can see the poet's eye for movement at work
as he describes what makes a toad's locomotion unique in a line
that itself sounds rather laboured and clumsy:

> You clamber towards me on your four corners —
> right hand, left foot, left hand, right foot.

Why doesn't he say 'right *foot*, left foot'? Does a toad have
hands?

There's a folk tradition that toads are wise and have a jewel
set in their brows — a special sign of favour, perhaps, in a little
animal more commonly supposed to be ugly, warty, and even
(wrongly) poisonous. For MacCaig, the uniqueness of the toad,
like its lack of fear, has put a jewel in *his* head — a small but
precious memory to set against the often bleaker and more disturbing facets of human consciousness — 'a tiny radiance in a
dark place'.

The ringed plover had its own uniqueness, too, and like the
toad it seems to MacCaig to be a focus for life itself. The bird
was a spot of light 'through a burning glass', and the toad sits
'directly under every star'. These lines suggest another reason
why animals are so important to the writer. They are somehow
in the centre of things for him — sparks of light and energy in
surrounding darkness. The same insight informs 'Blackbird in a
sunset bush' (273) where 'Everything's in the sunset' but 'Only
the blackbird . . . / contemplates / what the sunset's in: / what
makes a flower ponderous / and breathes a mountain away'. For
the poet the answer to this conundrum ('what makes a flower
ponderous'?), is to be found in 'The gravity of beauty', with
the bird at the heart of the sunset, like a piece of (black) char-
coal at the heart of a fire. 'Blue tit on a string of peanuts' (336)
makes the same connection, and plays with our sense of scale
in the same way, as if the smallest of birds somehow contains all
the force of a volcano or 'four inches of hurricane':

> A cubic inch of some stars
> weighs a hundred tons — Blue tit,
> who could measure the power
> of your tiny spark of energy?

The person who tries to measure these things is, of course, the
poet, and it's the unselfconscious *energy* of pure being which
MacCaig so often admires in the animals around him. He even
uses animal imagery to talk about himself, as in the amusingly
wry poem, 'Ineducable me' (337), where he describes himself as

somehow still feeling clumsy and 'ineducable' in his relations
with the world:

> How I admire the eider duck that dives
> with a neat loop and no splash and the gannet that suddenly
> harpoons the sea. — I'm a guillemot
> that still dives
> in the first way it thought of: poke your head under
> and fly down.

That apparent clumsiness, or the sheer 'oddness' to be found in
the world, seems to be one of the things that MacCaig most
values in life. Consider, for example, this next poem.

> *My last word on frogs*
>
> People have said to me, *You seem to like frogs.*
> *They keep jumping into your poems.*
>
> I do. I love the way they sit,
> compact as a cat and as indifferent
> to everything but style, like a lady remembering
> to keep her knees together. And I love
> the elegant way they jump and
> the inelegant way they land.
> So human.
>
> I feel so close to them
> I must be froggish myself.
> I look in the mirror expecting to see
> a fairytale Prince.
>
> But no. It's just sprawling me,
> croaking away
> and swivelling my eyes around
> for the stealthy heron and his stabbing beak.   (349)

Is he talking about frogs? Or is he really talking about people?
Or about himself? If he's talking — at least partly — about himself, what do you think the heron represents at the end?

'... dreadful requiems'

Of course, these verses are greatly good-humoured, but there
are other animal poems which take us deeper and closer to that

'dark place'. Perhaps praise poems will always have a sense of
how fleeting excellence must be in a world forever at the mercy
of disease, time and death. In 1977, MacCaig wrote a little
sequence of these poems, with the Gaelic tradition very much in
mind: 'Praise of a collie'; 'Praise of a boat'; 'Praise of a thorn
bush' and 'Praise of a road' (301-3). All these, like the poems
we have been discussing, focus on surprise, delight and the
specially unique kinds of movement to be found in each subject. They all show MacCaig's characteristic wit, with his boat as
'awkward as a piano' when the tide is wrong, or a thorn bush
trapping stars at night, or his road 'skidding on your own stones /
round improbable corners and arriving safe'. But such energy, in
living creatures at least, cannot last forever. In 'Praise of a collie',
for all that Lassie 'flowed through fences like a piece of black
wind', there came a time when 'suddenly she was old and sick
and crippled . . . '. In her prime, though, she was full of strength,
and despite her small size and quiet nature, she shares the same
vital 'spark of energy' that the poet saw in that blue tit among
the peanuts, or in the stars themselves.

Praise of a collie

She was a small dog, neat and fluid —
Even her conversation was tiny:
She greeted you with *bow*, never *bow-wow*.

Her sons stood monumentally over her
But did what she told them. Each grew grizzled
Till it seemed he was his own mother's grandfather.

Once, gathering sheep on a showery day,
I remarked how dry she was. Pollochan said, "Ah,
It would take a very accurate drop to hit Lassie."

She sailed in the dinghy like a proper sea-dog.
Where's a burn? — she's first on the other side.
She flowed through fences like a piece of black wind.

But suddenly she was old and sick and crippled . . .
I grieved for Pollochan when he took her for a stroll
And put his gun to the back of her head.   (301)

So the natural world can bring darker premonitions. In
'Basking shark' (209), for example, the poet's little boat at sea

is bumped by a 'roomsized monster with a matchbox brain', and he feels as if he has been 'displaced', or hurled back to the beginnings of evolution:

> He displaced more than water. He shoggled me
> Centuries back — this decadent townee
> Shook on a wrong branch of his family tree.
>
> Swish up the dirt and, when it settles, a spring
> Is all the clearer. I saw me, in one fling,
> Emerging from the slime of everything.
>
> So who's the monster? ...

At first the poet's sense of security was shaken because he stubbed an oar 'on a rock where none should be', but more than that, his encounter with this huge shark (a sluggish beast over thirty feet long) has reminded him of the primitive origins of all life — including his own — in 'the slime of everything'.

In 'Found guilty' (316), the poet can only watch a sandpiper chick as it drowns and 'to this day, poor swimmer that I am, / it grieves me'. Or in 'Gin trap' (318), he comes across a hoodie crow badly maimed by a trap as it 'tries to stand, tries to fly':

> *Gin trap*
>
> In the wide bogland a hoodie crow
> six feet from the trap that had maimed him,
> tries to stand, tries to fly.
>
> In the rags of his feathers, with mad eyes,
> he surges about in the heather. Sometimes
> his frantic voice adds its ugliness
> to the terror and the pain.
>
> Little Lear, you have no Cordelia
> to lament for, no steepdown gulfs
> of liquid fire to burn you away
> into a cindery darkness.
>
> Your friends will come, your hoodie companions,
> with their dreadful requiems — or
> a gliding fox will tear you apart
> with his flashing, beautiful smile.

Why does the poet say the crow has no Cordelia? The reference is to Shakespeare's *King Lear*, and I think he mentions this in order to make us think about the differences between what happens in real life and what happens in art. The two are not the same. We may read about a 'tragic' plane crash in the newspapers, but it is not the stuff of high 'tragedy'. A great tragic play moves and even terrifies us, but its art also comforts us in some strange way, and we leave the theatre reassured that despite terrible suffering, the human spirit can still somehow rise above the awful things that happen to it.

So the mention of Cordelia suggests that the bird has no loved one to comfort him, like Lear's daughter, and hence there is no sign of beauty or charity in his little world. At the same time, a crow in a trap is not the stuff of great tragic art, and even although he flaps about like mad king Lear, dressed in rags on the stormy heath, he has no fine speeches to make, calling on the fiery heavens to end his suffering. All the crow can do is *add* to the ugliness of the scene with a 'frantic voice'. Lear's friends come to lament his death at the end of the play, but we can only wonder about this crow's friends. Why are their requiems 'dreadful'? Is it the harsh sound of their voices? Or perhaps we suspect that they have come to feed on their fellow when he dies? The poem ends even more grimly with a smile which is not the smile of friendship, but the 'flashing, beautiful' baring of teeth which will serve only to 'tear you apart'.

The crow is not alone, for just as many sad and randomly brutal things happen to human beings in this world, and there is not much dignity to them and no time for fine speeches.

These are some of the things that the poet cannot help noticing, among the 'many cargoes' which his senses bring to him. He explains that sometimes he feels like a 'Helpless collector' (355), with events bringing him presents which he cannot refuse:

> I'm the exultant possessor
> of the ones that please me. I try to be
> only the caretaker
> of the ones I hate.
>
> They won't let me.
>
> I put the crooked mask
> behind the delicate jar
> and it moves to the front.

The 'crooked mask', the ugly things in life, cannot be ignored
and sometimes they seem to overpower the 'delicate jar'. As
with the adder next to the butterfly, or the radio telling of 'tortures in foreign prisons' (in 'Equilibrist'), if the poet is to notice
things at all, he cannot escape seeing the pain of the world, as
well as its beauty. Yet the world is just the world, and quite in-
different to the drowned sandpiper or the trapped crow. It is
only man who worries about such things.

MacCaig develops his thoughts on this double vision in 'Two
focuses' (167). The poet begins by reminding a worm that it
cannot escape being eaten by the thrush, just as the stream will
soon be 'choked with salt' and lost in the sea. It's worth quoting
in full, and asking further questions about:

Two focuses

Blind worm, lasciviously stroking yourself through
damp grass, do you think to escape
the springheeled thrush or the wren,
that fusspot in green hedges?

Brown water, you'll lose
that peat stain, your throat
will be choked with salt, you
will entertain monsters.

Red stag, you'll be an old rug rotting in the heather,
or a bullet
will drop the whole world away
from under your feet.

Such dooms, and nothing to tremble for them
but the one human figure in the landscape
who, because he trembles for them,
is the one intruder.

I tremble for them. But death shrinks back again
into the beautiful forms of his disguises.
And I see only that mountain, this stream,
this pool, clipped between rocks like an agate.
And death and history hide behind
a rowan branch that
drags and skips and drags and skips
on the brown glass of water — on it
spin Christmas roses of foam.

Do the images applied to the worm make you think of anything other than just worms in the grass? If they do, why do
you think the poet wrote it like that? And what about the stag?
Supposedly it has been shot by a gun, but the images chosen
suggest a trapdoor and another kind of end. What kind of death
do they suggest and why do you think the poet wanted us to
think like that? Why is the human figure an 'intruder' just because he trembles for the fate of the animals? Finally, how does
the poem end? Sadly? Happily?

Most of these questions suggest their own answers if we read
the poem carefully enough. The last one is more complicated,
however, for I find the longer closing section both sad and
happy, and it's quite difficult to explain why. According to folk
belief, the rowan is a tree of good omen and useful for keeping
evil at bay. But the poet seems to say that its beauty is no more
than something for 'death' to hide behind. Yet the lines *are*
beautiful, and the intermittent touching of the branches on the
flowing stream is very finely observed and expressed — something static and beautiful making fleeting contact with something flowing and passing away — like time perhaps. Those
'Christmas roses' are just a way of describing the white foam
bells that sometimes accumulate where the water eddies in
burns. But the words 'Christmas' and 'roses' have such powerful
associations with hope, good cheer and beauty that the poem
ends with these feelings uppermost.

Yet 'death' and 'history' are still there, even if they are in
hiding. At other times when I read these lines the spinning foam
roses and that dragging and skipping motion seem less beautiful,
and imply instead a process which is merely erratic and futile.

The power of the words is that they can have many associations, and when poetry is working at its best it can assemble
these associations to affect us in rich and many-sided ways. Remember 'Equilibrist' and the poet's concern with the difficulty
of 'balancing' what he notices? Those closing lines in 'Two
focuses' seem to me to be balanced too, — finely and ambig-
uously — so that the presence of death in the world is celebrated
just as honestly as the abundance of beauty to be found all
around us.

' . . . croaking away and swivelling my eyes around'

This is not to say that MacCaig finds the world a gloomy
place. On the contrary, he finds constant illumination in the

most unlikely places. True humour is never blind to the darker shadows at the edge of things, and indeed without those shadows it would lose much of its savour. Consider his joking God-like pose at the end of 'Feeding ducks' (73), for example, in which his 'everlasting hand / Dropped on my hypocrite duck her grace of bread'. The lines suggest that some Christians see their God as the duck sees the poet. And then MacCaig adds his own perspective to the scene — that double vision again — and the poem ends on an ironic note that becomes a little sinister, but still with a light touch: 'And I thought, "The first to be fattened, the first to be dead", / Till my gestures enlarged, wide over the darkening land'.

MacCaig has written a number of directly humorous poems, such as '19th floor nightmare, New York' (313), in which a girl wakes from a nightmare in her skyscraper hotel, gasps with relief, and then looks out of the window 'straight / into the left eye of King Kong'. For the most part, however, his humour is less obvious, although it is still to be found in every poem he writes. A quiet humour is the very stuff of how he sees the world, and every metaphor he makes suggests there are new, surprising and entertaining connections to be made everywhere we look. In this way every one of his poems celebrates the 'cargoes' not just of our senses, but also of our minds. This is because it is in our minds that we see resemblances between things that we wouldn't normally link together. Making connections is the fundamental act of all intelligence. Of course the poet's skill is to make them for us, but if we didn't also see them in an instant, *and* get excited by them, his art would be meaningless.

Metaphorical connections, like the link between a purse and a toad discussed earlier, are at the heart of how MacCaig makes poems. We saw the same flair in his description of how guillemots dive ('poke your head under / and fly down'), or how frogs look when they are run over ('They die on roads / with arms across their chests and / heads high. . . . like Italian tenors' 143). He values these 'high absurdities' in his long autobiographical poem, 'A man in Assynt' (219), in which he visualises the whole animal kingdom from the heights to the depths, each with its own identity. And it is *his* identity, as a poet, to be constantly alert to them:

> These shapes, these incarnations, have their own determined
> identities, their own dark holiness, their
> high absurdities. See how they make

a breadth and assemblage of animals,
a perpendicularity of creatures, from where,
three thousand feet up, two ravens go by
in their seedy, nonchalant way, down to
the burn-mouth where baby mussels
drink fresh water through their beards —
or down, down still, to where the masked conger eel
goes like a gangster through
the weedy slums at the sea's foot.

Of course, MacCaig *invents* these characters for his creatures. Conger eels are not really 'gangsters' and few biologists would recognise young mussels as babies with beards. But MacCaig's art, like all art, is a matter of remaking the world as he sees it, and his most frequent impulse is to remake the world as a surprising and delightful place, full of irreverently *human* connections and insights. This makes almost all his poems 'praise' poems in which the most ordinary events become vividly different, as he explains at the end of his poem 'An ordinary day' (149): 'and my mind observed to me, / or I to it, how ordinary / extraordinary things are or / how extraordinary ordinary / things are, like the nature of the mind / and the process of observing'.

' . . . unpredictables and astonishments'

The same sense of humour makes MacCaig value everything that is unexpected and unruly in life. For him 'Every step / is a moonlanding, my feet sink / in unpredictables and astonishments' ('Inward bound', 252). In 'Centres of centres' (another of his rare autobiographical longer poems), he criticises those who would organise away both the comic and the tragic and the accidental in our lives. They would prefer us to forget:

the intrusion of the comic (see that sun, strolling over,
lordly magnifico, with a wig of cloud
slipping over one ear) — and of the tragic:
that whimsical water
lullabying in the sun can clench its fist
on the timbers it cradles.

In mid-air a gull peering down, bowed
between its wings,
unbows itself and cackles,
trips over the cackle and floats on;

and a baby boat
comically staggering across the bay
stops for a rest in the dead centre
of teeming unpredictables.   (236-7)

Thus it is that the poet's involvement with landscape has a lot to do with the discoveries that he makes there, for the unexpected is always popping up, whether he is in the countryside looking down on Glen Canisp (159), or trying to decipher 'the message' of Loch Rannoch with its 'hieroglyphs of light' (Landscape and I', 278). He can look at a mechanical digger on a building site in the city and see 'a clanking beast' in a 'swamp' ('Construction site', 137); or walk through Edinburgh on a windy day and find a policeman who 'Stands eighty degrees against the sky' ('Wind in the city', 138). When he travels abroad he is overwhelmed by new impressions and odd insights, so that he finds the 'extraordinary heads' from the paintings in the Uffizi gallery suddenly appearing all around him in the everyday Italian crowds ('The streets of Florence', 142).

Such insights are not always comfortable. In 'Hotel room, 12th floor' he looks out over New York to see the vast height of the Empire State Building reduced to 'a jumbo size dentist's drill', circled by a helicopter looking like 'a damaged insect', and he hears the 'warwhoops' of ambulances in 'glittering canyons and gulches', as if he were somehow out in the Wild West surrounded by Indians. Yet this is not a familiar Western movie, for it is a darker frontier out there, with 'harsh screaming from coldwater flats' and 'blood glazed on sidewalks'. Bright lights glare at night, but the poet still feels that 'midnight' (in a different sense) 'is not so easily defeated'. The cheerfully unlikely metaphors for a helicopter and a skyscraper which began the poem have turned to something darker by the end. And yet, when we think of it, those references to a dentist's drill and a wounded insect were hinting at pain and disgust from the very start. For MacCaig, the 'unpredictables' can be disturbing as well as entertaining. Yet he returns to a more optimistic outlook in 'The unlikely' (220), in which he explains that 'We like the unlikely. It's good / that the boundaries of the normal should be widened. / It means — how many things there are still to be noticed!'

Aunt Julia, Uncle Seamus and others

If MacCaig values the unexpected in his surroundings (and even looks for it) he likewise values the unexpected in people. He especially likes it when they upset or bypass our more conventional ways of behaving, speaking or thinking. In 'Country dance' (256), for example, he moves from a celebration of human energy to one of oddness itself:

Country dance

The room whirled and coloured
and figured itself with dancers.
Another gaiety seemed born of theirs
and flew like streamers
between their heads and the ceiling.

I gazed, coloured and figured,
down the tunnel of streamers —
and there, in the band, an old fiddler
sawing away in the privacy
of music. He bowed lefthanded and his right hand
was the wrong way round. Impossible.
But the jig bounced, the gracenotes
sparkled on the surface of the tune.
The odd man out, when it came to music,
was the odd man in.

There's a lesson here, I thought, climbing
into the pulpit I keep in my mind.
But before I'd said *Firstly brethren*, the tune
ended, the dancers parted, the old fiddler
took a cigarette from the pianist, stripped off
the paper and ate the tobacco.

The poet's 'Aunt Julia' (183), shares something of this chaotic energy:

Aunt Julia

Aunt Julia spoke Gaelic
very loud and very fast.
I could not answer her —
I could not understand her.

She wore men's boots
when she wore any.
— I can see her strong foot,
stained with peat,
paddling with the treadle of the spinning wheel
while her right hand drew yarn
marvellously out of the air.

Hers was the only house
where I've lain at night
in the absolute darkness
of a box bed, listening to
crickets being friendly.

She was buckets
and water flouncing into them.
She was winds pouring wetly
round house-ends.
She was brown eggs, black skirts
and a keeper of threepennybits
in a teapot.

Aunt Julia spoke Gaelic
very loud and very fast.
By the time I had learned
a little, she lay
silenced in the absolute black
of a sandy grave
at Luskentyre.
But I hear her still, welcoming me
with a seagull's voice
across a hundred yards
of peatscrapes and lazybeds
and getting angry, getting angry
with so many questions
unanswered.

(*Lazybeds:* small raised strips of cultivated land in the old
Highland style)

When the poet says he 'could not understand' Aunt Julia, do
you think he is referring only to her Gaelic? Certainly she
seems a disconcerting sort of person, with her dirty feet in

men's boots and a loud 'seagull's voice'! The poem is full of her
noisy and energetic spirit, and yet she herself is hardly described at all. What MacCaig gives us instead are isolated details
from the bustle of her daily round — she *was* 'buckets and
water', and 'winds pouring wetly' and 'brown eggs' and 'threepennybits / in a teapot'. These are just the sort of details a small
boy might notice — especially a boy unused to country life or
to how a spinning wheel works. Still, he was happy there in the
security of his bed, recessed in the wall, listening to the crickets.

But the poem itself is not quite so comfortable, and Aunt
Julia is still a bit disconcerting, for I think that the tone changes
towards the end. Do you sense this? How do you feel, for example, about the 'absolute darkness' of that box bed, compared
to the 'absolute black' of Julia's grave?

What has happened is that the author has grown up by the
time the poem ends. At last he can understand some of her
Gaelic, but now she is no longer there to speak it. Even so, he
imagines that he can still hear her, 'welcoming me', as if her
irrepressible spirit could call from beyond the grave. But why is
she getting angry, and what are those 'unanswered' questions? I
think they refer back to the kind of affectionate quizzing that
she would give him when he was a boy; but at the same time
they hint at bigger questions, perhaps, and to things that he still
cannot understand.

'Uncle Seamus' (184), is even more eccentric, while 'Mrs
Grant' (208), is a sadder and more unbalanced character. But
she, too, has a saving energy about her:

> She was a wild one, clutching in a fist
> (Made of green fingers once) whole crews of lost
> Norwegian sailors till half past four
> And up at six each with a woodpecker
> Inside his skull. She bred her blacktongued chows
> And starved them, and the Jerseys, while the glass
> Of gin was filled and filled.
>   . . .
>
> A Greek doom gathered round, the Furies whetted
> Their ugly beaks and one by one alighted
> On the rooftree . . . What of her was seen last
> Through the cracked windscreen of her blue Ford Eight
> Was a bruised cheek, a wild and staring eye . . .
> Her house (it's true) was called Society.

In the end, Mrs Grant runs away (or is driven off), Uncle
Seamus is taken away, and Aunt Julia dies. I think the writer is
concerned in these poems because with each person something
unique has been lost. (It might even be said that the strangeness
and the surprises of their inner worlds are only slightly odder
than what he so often sees in his owm imagination.)

People do not have to be eccentric, however, for MacCaig to
prize their uniqueness, for many of his poems deal with the
extra-ordinariness of perfectly ordinary characters. The poet
may be a well-known writer in Scotland's capital city, but his
Highland background has made him specially responsive to the
values of hospitality, sensitivity and understatement to be
found among those who live far from the sophisticated and
busy streets of Edinburgh. He knows too, that such values are
far from common in the modern world. This is exactly what he
describes in 'Return to Scalpay' (264):

> Edinburgh, Edinburgh, you're dark years away.
>
> Scuttering snowflakes riddling the hard wind
> Are almost spent
> When we reach Johann's house. She fills the doorway,
> Sixty years of size and astonishment,
> Then laughs and cries and laughs, as she always did
> And will (Easy glum, easy glow, a friend would say) . . .
> Scones, oatcakes, herrings from under a bubbling lid.
> Then she comes with us to put us on our way.
>
> Hugging my arm in her stronger one, she says,
> *Fancy me*
> *Walking this road beside my darling Norman!*
> And what is there to say? . . .

Almost everything that MacCaig values in human relationships
has come to him from this culture, and yet these values have
been greatly threatened by outside pressures. General economic
forces, the Clearances, or the more recent transactions of private
landowners have done much to depopulate the Highlands over
the years, and the poet asks some angry questions about this
fact in 'A man in Assynt':

> Who owns this landscape? —
> The millionaire who bought it or
> the poacher staggering downhill in the early morning
> with a deer on his back?

Who possesses this landscape? —
The man who bought it or
I who am possessed by it?
. . .

Or has it come to this,
that this dying landscape belongs
to the dead, the crofters and fighters
and fishermen whose larochs
sink into the bracken
by Loch Assynt and Loch Crocach? —
to men trampled under the hooves of sheep
and driven by deer to
the ends of the earth — to men whose loyalty
was so great it accepted their own betrayal
by their own chiefs and whose descendants now
are kept in their place
by English businessmen and the indifference
of a remote and ignorant government.   (214-5)

(*laroch:* the remains of an old building)

MacCaig doesn't often make direct political comments like
this, but he refers again to the bitter history of the Highland
Clearances in his poem 'Two thieves' (359). For the most part,
however, his poems are firmly focused on the here-and-now,
and on his own immediate experience. Thus he acknowledges a
personal debt to Gaelic culture in his lasting love of pibroch —
the classical music of the Highland bagpipe — and by remembering childhood visits to Scalpay when he was:

. . . a millionaire of sunlight and summer winds,
freeman of kingdoms behind a kingdom,
far traveller among spinningwheels,
explorer of songs,
and without knowing it a miser
stuffing the bag of my mind
with sovereigns
I've been spending ever since.   ('Inward bound', 251)

When you are young it seems as if such riches will last forever,
but the poet has written other verses which recognise that what
he loves in Highland culture may some day pass away. One of
the most sustained expressions of this insight is to be found in

the moving sequence 'Poems for Angus' (320), which was written after the death of his old friend, Angus K. MacLeod.

'AK' lived in Inverkirkaig where the poet spent his summers for many years. When his friend died, it seemed to Norman MacCaig as if the heart of the place had been somehow taken away.

A.K. MacLeod

I went to the landscape I love best
and the man who was its meaning and added to it
met me in Ullapool.

The beautiful landscape was under snow
and was beautiful in a new way.

Next morning the man who had greeted me
with the pleasure of pleasure
vomited blood
and died.

Crofters and fishermen and womenfolk, unable
to say any more, said,
'It's a grand day, it's a beautiful day.'

And I thought, 'Yes it is'.
And I thought of him lying there,
the dead centre of it all.

MacCaig achieves a new bareness of expression in these moving poems, and his own unwillingness 'to say any more' comes across very powerfully in the use of understated and curiously impersonal phrases such as 'the man who had greeted me'. Here, too, he places what is most dear to him somehow at the centre of things. Look again at this poem (and its fellows) and ask yourself what I mean by saying that they show a new 'bareness' in expression.

'. . . the dead centre of it all'

The 'Poems to Angus' seem to me to be among MacCaig's finest explorations of the theme of mortality. An awareness of mortality has always been part of his art for, once again, it seems likely that 'praise poems' must always imply the possibility of future loss. Even so, the death of A.K. MacLeod, like the

earlier death of the poet's friend Hugh MacDiarmid, has brought
MacCaig to write in his later years a number of finely economical
and elegiac poems. (See, for example, 'Two friends', 334). His
own experience of advancing age has given added force to such
feelings, ('Fisherman, 338); as has his wife's encounter with
cancer in a poem such as 'It's come to this' (350), which appears
again as 'Her illness' followed, more happily, by 'End of her
illness', in the 1988 collection *Voice Over.*

It is significant that when he thinks of death, MacCaig sees
a grey and featureless condition, a landscape, for once, without
the possibilities of surprise and delight that he finds at every
turn in this world. In 'Angus's dog' (323) it is a 'blank no-time,
no-place where / you can't even greet your master / though he's
there too'; while 'In that other world' (375), describes a terrify-
ingly bland location, like the inside of a long burial mound, perhaps, or some ghastly committee room:

In that other world

They sit at their long table
in a room so long it's a tunnel,
in a tunnel with a green roof
on which sometimes a flower nods
as if to remind them of something.

They talk about everything
except Death, but they don't listen
to each other. They talk, staring
straight in front of them.
And they tremble.

The only time they notice each other
is when Death sweeps past them
with his keys clinking and a long pen
in his hand.

Then they look shyly at each other
for a moment before staring ahead
and talking, talking, trying to remember
what a flower is,
trying to remember
why they are here.

It's not the suffering that makes this vision frightening for me,

but all the boredom of a waiting room where you have forgotten
what you are waiting for. Is it like a hospital waiting room? Or
a station, or a prison, or some vast office corridor? Why is
Death carrying a pen?

The same sense of boredom and despair can be found in
'Blind horse' (167), and although MacCaig is writing about an
animal in this poem, it seems to me that he has a special personal sympathy for a creature which has been deprived of the
world and all the everyday delights which it brings to our attention. Without such stimulation the horse has no relish in eating
or drinking, his field will always be 'dark' as he waits impatiently
for the light and 'whinnies / for what never comes'.

These poems complete the understanding that MacCaig describes in 'The unlikely', where he celebrates 'how many things
there are still to be noticed', only to recognise that life offers
harsher insights as well, about 'how many things there are still
to be suffered!' (221). In this respect the poem 'Assisi' (150),
conveys great compassion for the human condition. But there
is a darker irony to be found there, too.

Assisi

The dwarf with his hands on backwards
sat, slumped like a half-filled sack
on tiny twisted legs from which
sawdust might run,
outside the three tiers of churches built
in honour of St Francis, brother
of the poor, talker with birds, over whom
he had the advantage
of not being dead yet.

A priest explained
how clever it was of Giotto
to make his frescoes tell stories
that would reveal to the illiterate the goodness
of God and the suffering
of his Son. I understood
the explanation and
the cleverness.

A rush of tourists, clucking contentedly,
fluttered after him as he scattered

the grain of the Word. It was they who had passed
the ruined temple outside, whose eyes
wept pus, whose back was higher
than his head, whose lopsided mouth
said *Grazie* in a voice as sweet
as a child's when she speaks to her mother
or a bird's when it spoke
to St Francis.

It's not easy to put your finger on MacCaig's irony in this poem,
and yet I'm sure every reader will feel something of his sup-
pressed anger that such suffering should have to exist in our
world, and that our institutions (in this case, the Church)
should be failing to make things better.

Each stanza ends with a wry twist — the dwarf has an 'advantage' over St Francis in 'not being dead yet'. Yet look at
how the poor fellow is described. Does this sound 'alive'? In the
next stanza, the poet understands 'the explanation and / the
cleverness', but does he understand 'the goodness / of God and
the suffering / of His Son'? Finally, the closing images of a
child and its mother, or a bird and St Francis, bring associations
of innocence, mutual love, trust and dependence. Are these
quite the right terms for the dwarf beggar's relationship to those
whom he is thanking for their charity? He says *Grazie*, after all,
in a sweet voice, so why does this not seem to be a kindly trans-
action?

The answer, I think, is to be found in the wider context.
The tourists seem more interested in the priest's talk than they
are in the beggar — they passed him by, after all, on their way
into the church to see wall paintings done by Giotto, the famous
Italian Renaissance artist. So the tourists are 'clucking contentedly', like birds themselves, pecking up the 'grain of the Word',
as if Christian faith were food to satisfy their hunger. Yet the
beggar is in need of real food and neither words nor 'the Word'
itself will fill his belly. Another poet might have written that
the beggar found comfort in his faith, but MacCaig does not
allow us to consider this. Instead he makes a striking parallel
between 'the three tiers of churches built / in honour of St
Francis', and 'the ruined temple outside'. The ruined temple
is, of course, the dwarf himself, the 'temple' of whose body is
weeping pus and twisted all out of shape. It's difficult to for-
give the tourists for 'clucking' so 'contentedly' in front of
such a contrast.

Finally, the whole scene seems to be turned-in on itself: St
Francis talked to the birds. The priest talks about St Francis to
the tourists (who listen like birds). The dwarf thanks the tourists for their charity (like a bird talking to St Francis). It's all
circular, somehow, and there seems to be (despite all the talking)
no answer and no way out. St Francis's message was about the
brotherhood of all living beings, but MacCaig can see little
enough evidence of this, and he is left instead with irony and a
barely hidden gentle rage. I find a similar anger at the suffering
that God (seemingly) allows his creatures to endure in poems
such as 'The Kirk' (332), and 'Yes' (371).

What is there to set against such darkness? Well, in Norman
MacCaig's case, of course, the physical world still offers the
promise of constant fascination and creative renewal. He may
have difficulty at times in balancing 'tortures in foreign prisons'
against 'a sonata of Schubert', but by far the greater part of his
work celebrates a human delight in music, companionship and
the workings of nature.

' . . . returning to the marvellous world of possibility'

MacCaig has written love poems in which the lady of his
affections sometimes appears as herself, and sometimes as, at
least partly, a figure of the Muse, who stands for all that is
positive and fine in human feeling — although that feeling can
be destructive, too. In 'I and my thoughts of you' (244), the
poet compares himself to an 'old thorn bush / amazed by / its
one flower' when he thinks of his love; while 'Incident' (231),
describes the sweet pain of wanting to do more than can be
done for someone for whom you care:

Incident

I look across the table and think
(fiery with love)
Ask me, go on, ask me
to do something impossible,
something freakishly useless,
something unimaginable and inimitable

like making a finger break into blossom
or walking for half an hour in twenty minutes
or remembering tomorrow.

> I will you to ask it.
> But all you say is
> Will you give me a cigarette, please?
> And I smile and,
> returning to the marvellous world
> of possibility,
> I give you one
> with a hand that trembles
> with a human trembling.

The poem is typically witty, but those last lines are very important to what it's saying, and they seem to shift to a more serious note at the end. Why do you think this should be?

In other poems MacCaig's Muse-lover brings him up against the constant search to write well enough to do justice to them both, as he realises in 'To explain you' (319).

> I look for the answer, the one simple answer
> among the so many,
> that would explain you to me. I can't find it.
>
> Am I a fool? Am I looking in the wrong places?

The same struggle with expression is the subject of 'Words in nowhere' (241), for all poets fear the loss of inspiration and it is hard work to bring their images into the light:

> With you not here what have I not to say?
> I beat my mind dazed in the space between us.
> — I'd write you; but the words have gone away.
>
> The words gone? No: they bulge so in my net
> I can't haul them up from the great depth between us
> No matter how the stretched ropes fray and fret. . . .

Even if inspiration strikes, MacCaig is sceptical enough to question that curious balance between the creative urge itself and the need to tell the truth — not least in a love poem! This is the subject of 'A man in my position' (200), which imagines a separation between the man who loves and the man who writes about it:

> Hear my words carefully.
> Some are spoken
> not by me, but
> by a man in my position.

Divided between the 'man' and the 'poet', MacCaig ends by
wondering 'who is talking now?'. And he recognises that sometimes his loved one must ask herself this too, even if 'he loves
you also, / this appalling stranger / who makes windows of my
eyes'.

These themes — personal affection and the compulsion to
write — come together in a beautiful poem called 'No choice'
(191):

> *No choice*
>
> I think about you
> in as many ways as rain comes.
>
> (I am growing, as I get older,
> to hate metaphors — their exactness
> and their inadequacy.)
>
> Sometimes these thoughts are
> a moistness, hardly falling, than which
> nothing is more gentle:
> sometimes, a rattling shower, a
> bustling Spring-cleaning of the mind:
> sometimes a drowning downpour.
>
> I am growing, as I get older,
> to hate metaphor,
> to love gentleness,
> to fear downpours.

Why do you think he fears 'downpours' as he gets older? And
what might the 'drowning downpour' represent? Too much
feeling? Is he talking about poetry, or about love? Or both?

The poet might be a little wary of metaphor in these particular verses, but metaphors or similes still lie at the absolute
centre of MacCaig's creative method. When he sees a swan in
'Inward bound', for example, it appears to him 'floating like a
lotus / with a white snake in it' (253). Thus what is a familiar
sight to our eyes is made new and challenging and fresh again.
The thought of that flower of peace and tranquillity with a
'white snake' inside it, is even a little strange and frightening.
This is how poetry — and painting too — has always worked to
encourage, or renew, our creative involvement with everything
we see around us.

POETRY: 'YOU, DECORATOR AND DISTURBER ... '

So, in the end, we come down to poetry itself. Take away MacCaig's enjoyment of animals and landscape, take away his delight in the unpredictable, and his care for ordinary people and the plain values of everyday Highland life; take away even his compassion for human suffering and for the fact that death is final and inescapable; remove all these, and the poet is still left with the 'riches' of words and the lively stimulation of the creative act itself:

> *Elemental you*
>
> As the rain makes
> Blue gold-shines on the puddled mud at gates
> And tinily trickles over small estates
>
> And as the wind
> Hullabaloos a tree against its will
> To stop the nonsense of just standing still,
>
> On any day
> You, decorator and disturber, make
> Me unexpected: my gray turns crimson lake,
>
> My thoughts that are
> Great liers on their backs get up and dance
> And my face shines, though I lose countenance
>
> Being forced to agree
> Mud can be trampled bright and — look at me!
> I can dance too, if only like a tree.   (234)

This seems such a simple little piece, with simple rhymes, and yet there are a number of questions worth asking about it. Why does he put 'elemental' in the title? Is he thinking of *the* elements (which elements?) or 'elemental spirits'? Why is 'just standing still' a 'nonsense'? And why does he spend so much time thinking of mud and puddles — not very beautiful things, surely? (Yet even mud can be made 'bright' when it is 'trampled'. Is he thinking of his own troubles?) Why does he 'lose countenance' when he finds himself forced to dance? In the end the poet seems to me to be like an old tree, forced by the wind, and perhaps by inspiration to liven himself up on a blustery day.

MacCaig has written a number of poems about poetry or about making art, and they bring us back to the acts of celebration and praise which are fundamental to his verse, and a part of what all artists have always sought to do. He himself is humorously modest about how he writes, but this does not mean that his writing is less than wholly serious.

> When I feel like writing a poem, I sit down with a blank sheet of paper and no idea whatever in my head. Into it, where there's plenty of room, enters the memory of a place, an emotional experience, a person, or, most commonly, a phrase, and the poem stalactites down the page from that. This means I'm into the poem, various distances, before I know what it's about. In fact I don't know what the poem's about till I've finished it. This sounds daft, but I believe it's a common enough experience with poets. . . .
>
> My notions about the value of poetry and the ways it is produced are, I've come to notice, fairly low-falutin'. I never met a White Goddess in my life and when I find myself in the company of singing robes, hieratic gestures and fluting voices, I phone a taxi. The pleasure in making poems lies in making them and seems to me not different from a true craftsman's pleasure in making a table. . . .
>
> ('My Way of It')

Of course, MacCaig is making poems and not tables. Are poems functional, however, in the way that tables are? Or are they just to entertain us and their maker? (Not that there's anything wrong with that, of course.)

In one of his poems about painting, 'Still life' (99), MacCaig suggests that even the most undramatic subject can have an extraordinary creative power:

> *Still life*
>
> Three apples, if they are apples, and a jug,
> A lemon (certain), grapes, a fish's tail,
> A melting fruitdish and a randy table:
> Squared off from other existences they struggle
> Into a peace, a balancing of such power
> As past and future use in being Now.

Still life, they call it — like a bursting bomb
That keeps on bursting, one burst, on and on:
A new existence, continually being born,
Emerging out of white into the sombre
Garishness of the spectrum, refusing the easy,
Clenching its strength on nothing but how to be.

Nice lesson for a narrative or for
A thing made emblem — that martyrs in their fire,
Christs on their crosses, fetes and massacres,
When purified of their small history,
Cannot surpass, no matter how they struggle,
Three apples (more than likely) and a jug.

What *is* the force behind that bursting bomb? A force so powerful, that martyrs, massacres and crucifixions seem like 'small
history' by comparison?

Well, I think the still life tells us about two things, really,
apart, that is, from simply depicting some fruit and a jug. The
first is the power of the human imagination which made the
picture, 'squared off from other existences' and balanced by
the artist's craft. (I think that he is looking at a cubist work.)
The paintings, like MacCaig's metaphors about a swan or a
toad, makes us see how extraordinary the ordinary can be. That
is, our imagination has the power to transform the world by
transforming *how we see it*. In this respect, art and literature
can be a great influence in the world of affairs, because history
shows us that men fight over ideas and how they feel about
them at least as much as they do over economics or material
gain.

The second thing the still life tells us about, is the nature
of 'Now', which is the abstract nature of existence itself,
emerging out of white blankness and focused on 'nothing but
how to be'. We look at an ordinary apple and nothing much
strikes us. But in the eyes of the poet, the painter or the philo-
sopher it's like a bomb going off, something so intensely itself
that it's almost frightening. Once seen in this imaginative light,
all created things — even the meanest — become special. (I
think that this is one of the reasons why MacCaig likes animals
so much, for they only know the here-and-now — being entirely
and unselfconsciously themselves.)

The same insight about art appears in another piece called
'Painting — "The Blue Jar" ' (189), in which the poet admires

'the muscles of pigments / that can hold out a jar for years / without trembling'. Yet making art can be strenuous and diffi-cult, for language is slippery and sometimes 'the words have gone away'. Nevertheless, the drive to express ourselves, and the drive to understand things emotionally as well as intellectually is crucial. Writing of 'the special, unique and practical import-ance of poetry and the other arts', MacCaig explains:

> The nub and centre (pith, if you like) of my thinking about that is this: An adult physique with the intelligence of a child is looked upon as potentially dangerous. But an adult intelligence along with the emotional equipment of a child is even more so. Intellect and sensibility — the arts develop both. Poetry teaches a man to do more than observe merely factual errors and meas-urable truths. It trains him to have a shrewd nose for the fake, the inflated, the imprecise and the dishonest. So, it compels him to resist stock responses, because it compels him to examine the emotional significance, as well as the rational significance, of whatever comes under his notice. To have unexamined emotional responses is as immature, as dangerous, as to have unexamined be-liefs. And what proportion, I wonder, of the misunderstandings and miseries in the world are due to no more than the stock use of big words — liberty, patriotism, democracy and all their dreary clan — and the stock response to them?

('My Way of It')

The poet's dislike of 'big words' comes across in 'A man I agreed with' (317), a poem which sums up his own open accept-ance of the wonders of ordinary experience just as it is, as if they were a kind of test for what is truly authentic, as opposed to mankind's more high-faluting abstractions and pretensions. He seems to be talking about a friend, but he could easily be speaking of himself:

> *A man I agreed with*
>
> He knew better than to admire a chair
> and say *What does it mean?*
>
> He loved everything that accepted
> the unfailing hospitality of his five senses.
> He would say *Hello, caterpillar* or
> *So long, Loch Fewin.*

He wanted to know
how they came to be what they are:
But he never insulted them by saying,
Caterpillar, Loch Frewin, what do you mean?

In this respect he was like God,
though he was godless. — He knew the difference
between *What does it mean to me?*
and *What does it mean?*

That's why he said, half smiling,
Of course, God, like me,
is an atheist.

Atheist he may be, but Norman MacCaig speaks for the holiness
of the everyday world in every one of his poems. He seizes the
fleeting moment in his verse in order to transform it, or to reveal it, in an affirmative act of praise and endless celebration.
The celebration is endless because the poet's art lives on, long
after what inspired it has changed or passed away. And the celebration is endless because ordinary life goes on, and there is
always delight to be found there, if only we have eyes to see.

Notations of ten summer minutes

A boy skips flat stones out to sea — each does fine
till a small wave meets it head on and swallows it.
The boy will do the same.

The schoolmaster stands looking out of the window
with one Latin eye and one Greek one.
A boat rounds the point in Gaelic.

Out of the shop comes a stream
of Omo, Weetabix, BiSoDol tablets and a man
with a pocket shaped like a whisky bottle.

Lord V. walks by with the village in his pocket.
Angus walks by
spending the village into the air.

A melodeon is wheezing a clear-throated jig
on the deck of the *Arcadia*. On the shore hills Pan
cocks a hairy ear; and falls asleep again.

The ten minutes are up, except they aren't.
I leave the village, except I don't.
The jig fades to silence, except it doesn't.

NOTES

1   These and all following autobiographical quotations come from
     Norman MacCaig, 'My Way of It', in *As I Remember*, ed. M. Lindsay
     (London: Robert Hale Ltd., 1979), pp. 81-8.

2   'Return to landscape', from *The Inward Eye* (London, 1946), p. 41.

3   Hugh MacDiarmid, *The Company I've Kept* (London: Hutchinson,
     1966), p. 235.

4   Norman MacCaig, quoted in *Worlds: Seven Modern Poets*, ed. G.
     Summerfield (London, 1974), p. 162.

5   *The Songs of Duncan Ban Macintyre*, ed. and trans. Angus MacLeod
     (Edinburgh: Scottish Gaelic Text Society, 1952), p. 169.

6   See for example: 'Praise of a collie', 301, 'Angus's dog', 323; 'Byre',
     98, 'Fetching cows', 117, 'Bull', 115, 'Running bull', 367; 'Blind
     horse', 167; 'Goat', 67; 'Stag in a neglected hayfield', 272; 'Cock
     before dawn', 340, 'Feeding ducks', 73; 'Wild oats', 221; 'Solitary
     crow', 182; 'Four o'clock blackbird', 156, 'Blackbird in a sunset
     bush', 273; 'Starlings', 170, 'Starling on a green lawn', 347; 'Spar-
     row', 246; 'Bargain with a wren', 227; 'Blue tit on a string of pea-
     nuts', 336; 'Bullfinch on guard in a hawthorn tree', 383; 'Stonechat
     on Cul Beg', 297; 'Greenshank', 271; 'Waxwing', 293; 'Gray wagtail',
     353; 'Ringed plover by a water's edge', 267; 'Gulls on a hill loch',
     247; 'Cormorants nesting', 328; 'Puffin', 342; 'Kingfisher', 298;
     'Preening swan', 279; 'Porpoises', 144; 'Basking shark', 209; 'Whales',
     166; 'Caterpillar', 227, 'Caterpillar going somewhere', 271; 'Ear-
     wig', 342; 'Swimming lizard', 20; 'Jumping toad', 314, 'Toad', 336;
     'Frogs', 143, 'One of the many days', 204, 'My last word on frogs',
     349.

APPENDIX 1
PRACTICAL CRITICISM

You may want to try some slightly more demanding exercises in practical criticism. Once again, it's helpful to ask questions -- the right questions — as a way into a fuller understanding of any creative work, and you should keep the poem in front of you as you read these notes.

The following three poems are subtle in their effects, and it's not always easy to see or to say why. Yet every detail on the page contributes something vital to how we feel, and therefore to what we know about the poem.

The first two examples show us how a poet can actively make connections across what may at first sight seem to be merely random details in an ordinary scene. In this way the poem becomes a rounded work of art, even if it seems to be simply describing a few real events just as they happened. In other words, poets may well use the material of real life, but they choose it, or re-organise it, or express it in such a way as to begin to say extra or even entirely new things about the experience.

Look again at 'Notations of ten summer minutes' (pp. 40-1).

Notice how the poet sets lines and images against other lines and images. Either they link up, or they make some sort of contrast. This can be seen at work in the first two stanzas:

First of all, there's the boy and the skipping stone. What does the poet mean by 'The boy will do the same?' It suggests that the boy and the flat stone have something in common. What is it?

Then there's the schoolmaster and the boat. Do they have anything in common. If so, what is it? If not, why not?

The next image makes a link between the third and fourth stanzas via the repetition of the word 'pocket'.

Who is the man with a whisky bottle in his pocket, and who is the man with the village in his pocket? In what ways are they different from each other?

Finally, in the second last stanza:

Why is the boat called *Arcadia*? Who is Pan and what has he got to do with the boat? Is it significant that Pan is asleep?

Looking over the poem as a whole:

What sort of place is this? What sort of day has it been? Why does the poet include Omo, Weetabix and BiSoDol tablets? Could he have chosen other products? Think of some completely different ones and see if it changes anything.

The next example is a sadder poem. Perhaps here something really has come to a stop.

Interruption to a journey

The hare we had run over
bounced about the road
on the springing curve
of its spine.

Cornfields breathed in the darkness.
We were going through the darkness and
the breathing cornfields from one
important place to another.

We broke the hare's neck
and made that place, for a moment,
the most important place there was,
where a bowstring was cut
and the bow broken for ever
that had shot itself through so many
darknesses and cornfields.

It was left in that landscape.
It left us in another.   (144)

First of all, a question about what actually happened.

Did they kill the hare outright with the car, or did they have to give it a mercy killing?

And now a series of questions about how the poet has organised the experience by choosing and repeating certain words.

What particular image is associated with the hare? What words are repeated throughout the poem?

Why do 'bow' and 'bowspring' seem appropriate?

Why does he talk about the cornfields 'breathing'?

We know the incident happened at night, but is this why the word 'darkness' appears three times?

Look at how he repeats the word 'important'. Do you sense a change of tone — that is, in the poet's attitude to the notion of importance — between the two instances?

Why was that place, even for a moment, 'the most important place there was'? Who was it important to?

Look at the poem's title again. How do you feel about it now?

What do the last two lines tell us?

I think that this is an extraordinarily powerful little poem. It seems to be expressed in the plainest terms, and yet it says far more than it seems to, and it does it more effectively than a more obviously emotional piece would.

The third and last example takes us back to MacCaig's poems about human suffering. In happier pieces he used his skills to make the world seem suddenly fresh and unusual, but in this poem things seem strange and threatening instead. Even so, it is the same process of transformation at work.

Visiting hour

The hospital smell
combs my nostrils
as they go bobbing along
green and yellow corridors.

What seems a corpse
is trundled into a lift and vanishes
heavenward.

I will not feel, I will not
feel, until
I have to.

Nurses walk lightly, swiftly,
here and up and down and there,
their slender waists miraculously
carrying their burden
of so much pain, so
many deaths, their eyes
still clear after
so many farewells.

Ward 7. She lies
in a white cave of forgetfulness.
A withered hand
trembles on its stalk. Eyes move
behind eyelids too heavy
to raise. Into an arm wasted
of colour a glass fang is fixed,
not guzzling but giving.
And between her and me
distance shrinks till there is none left
but the distance of pain that neither she nor I
can cross.

She smiles a little at this
black figure in her white cave
who clumsily rises
in the round swimming waves of a bell
and dizzily goes off, growing fainter,
not smaller, leaving behind only
books that will not be read
and fruitless fruits.   (173)

This poem is full of nightmarish distortions, and odd ways
of saying things.

Consider those smells 'combing' the poet's nostrils. And
notice that it's not the speaker who goes 'bobbing along' the
corridor, but his *nostrils*.

It's as if smells and nostrils could have a life of their own.

After the poet's 'nostrils', look at how the person he is
visiting is described. Do you see any similarities?

There is only '*a* withered hand', trembling on a 'stalk'.
What does this make you think of?

Then there are 'eyes' and 'an arm', and the intravenous

drip becomes 'a glass fang', almost as much a part of the lady (or *not* a part of her) as that hand and those 'eyes that move behind eyelids'.

The poet walks closer to the bed, but is this what he says? What he says is 'between her and me / distance shrinks'. Or is he talking only about physical distance? What other kinds of distance does he mention?

Everything is de-personalised somehow. Why?

In the confusion of the hospital and in the confusion of his own feelings, the poet feels strangely apart from everything, including himself.

He snatches at impressions, and they're not very comfortable ones. A corpse, or what *'seems'* a corpse 'vanishes / heavenward'.

Why say 'heavenward'?

Nurses walk 'here and up and down and there'. Surely this is a very clumsy line to find in a poem?

Why call a needle a 'fang'? And since it's 'giving' and not 'guzzling', why mention 'guzzling' in the first place?

Why describe the bed and its curtains as a 'white cave of forgetfulness'?

Who is the 'black figure' in that 'white cave'? Why say 'black figure'?

Why are the fruits 'fruitless'?

The figure goes off 'clumsily' and 'dizzily' as if floating away 'in the round swimming waves of a bell'.

What bell? And just who is feeling like this — the patient or the visitor?

I think the last verse is written from the patient's 'dizzy' point of view, but in fact the whole poem has been so oddly dislocated that both patient and visitor seem to be swimming — or bobbing — through a kind of sea.

Why do you think MacCaig has chosen to distort the whole poem like this? Why might the patient be feeling dizzy? And why the visitor?

There are, perhaps, a few lines in the poem where the poet does speak for himself, simply and plainly. Compared to the rest, it almost comes as a shock.

> Which are these lines? Do they help to explain what has
> been going on?

APPENDIX 2
POETRY DISCUSSED

Poems discussed complete are in capitals; the rest are dealt with in significant detail, passing references are not included. Starred titles are also to be found on the cassette tape ASLS Commentary 9, *Nineteen Poems of Norman MacCaig*, with Professor Edwin Morgan and Norman MacCaig.

SELECT BIBLIOGRAPHY

Norman MacCaig, 'My Way of It', first published in *Chapman*, 16, 1976 and collected in *As I Remember*, ed. Maurice Lindsay (London: Robert Hale Ltd, 1979).

Marshal Walker, interview with Norman MacCaig in *Seven Poets* (Glasgow: Third Eye Centre, 1981).

Raymond J. Ross, interview with Norman MacCaig in *Cencrastus*, 8, Spring 1982.

Iain Crichton Smith, 'The Poetry of Norman MacCaig', *Saltire Review*, VI, 19, 1959.

Akros, III, 7, March 1968, 'Special Norman MacCaig Issue'.

Robin Fulton, 'Ishmael Among the Phenomena', *Scottish International*, V, 8, 1972.

Robin Fulton, 'Norman MacCaig', in *Contemporary Scottish Poetry. Individuals and Contexts* (Loanhead: Macdonald, 1974).

John Herdman, 'Metaphor and Mortality', *Scotia Rampant*, 5, Winter 1985, 'Norman MacCaig Issue'.

Thomas Crawford, 'Norman MacCaig: Makar Compleit'; and Iain Crichton Smith, 'A Lust for the Particular', both in *Chapman*, 45, Summer 1986, 'Special Feature on Norman MacCaig'.

For wider contexts see also:

Alan Bold, *Modern Scottish Literature* (London: Longman, 1983).

Roderick Watson, *The Literature of Scotland* (London: Macmillan, 1984).

John Blackburn, *Hardy to Heaney -- Twentieth Century Poets* (Oliver and Boyd, 1986).